Standin' Tall® with SELF-ESTEEM

Music by
Janeen Brady
Script by
Diane Woolley and Janeen Brady

Series Includes
1. Obedience
2. Honesty
3. Forgiveness
4. Work
5. Courage
6. Happiness
7. Gratitude
8. Love
9. Service
10. Cleanliness
★11. Self-Esteem
12. Dependability

©Copyright 1984 by Janeen Brady. All rights reserved. No part of this book may be reproduced in any form. Printed in the United States of America.

Emily, what's wrong?

★**I don't have any friends. Nobody likes me.**

I like you.

★**How could anyone like me?**

Oh, Emily, thinking you haven't any friends reminds me of a little boy I once knew named Mark.

★**Who's Mark?**

He was a little boy just about your age. It all started one day when his class went to the zoo.

CHILDREN: We're here! We're at the zoo! I can see the giraffe. Where's the monkey cage?

TEACHER: Stay together, children. Now, be sure to hold hands with your partner.

★★**I don't have a partner. I didn't want to come to the old zoo, anyway. It's no fun to be at the zoo all by yourself.**

Everybody needs a friend, yes, they do.
Everybody needs a friend who is true
(But I don't have a friend)—
A special friend who puts them at ease,
A special friend in whom they believe.
(I wish I had a friend.)

Everybody needs a friend, it's a fact—
(It's a fact. It's a fact.)
Someone they can trust who won't turn their back
(When I need him the most),
Someone they really like a lot,
Someone who makes them smile—
A special friend, (Squawk, Squawk) a special friend.

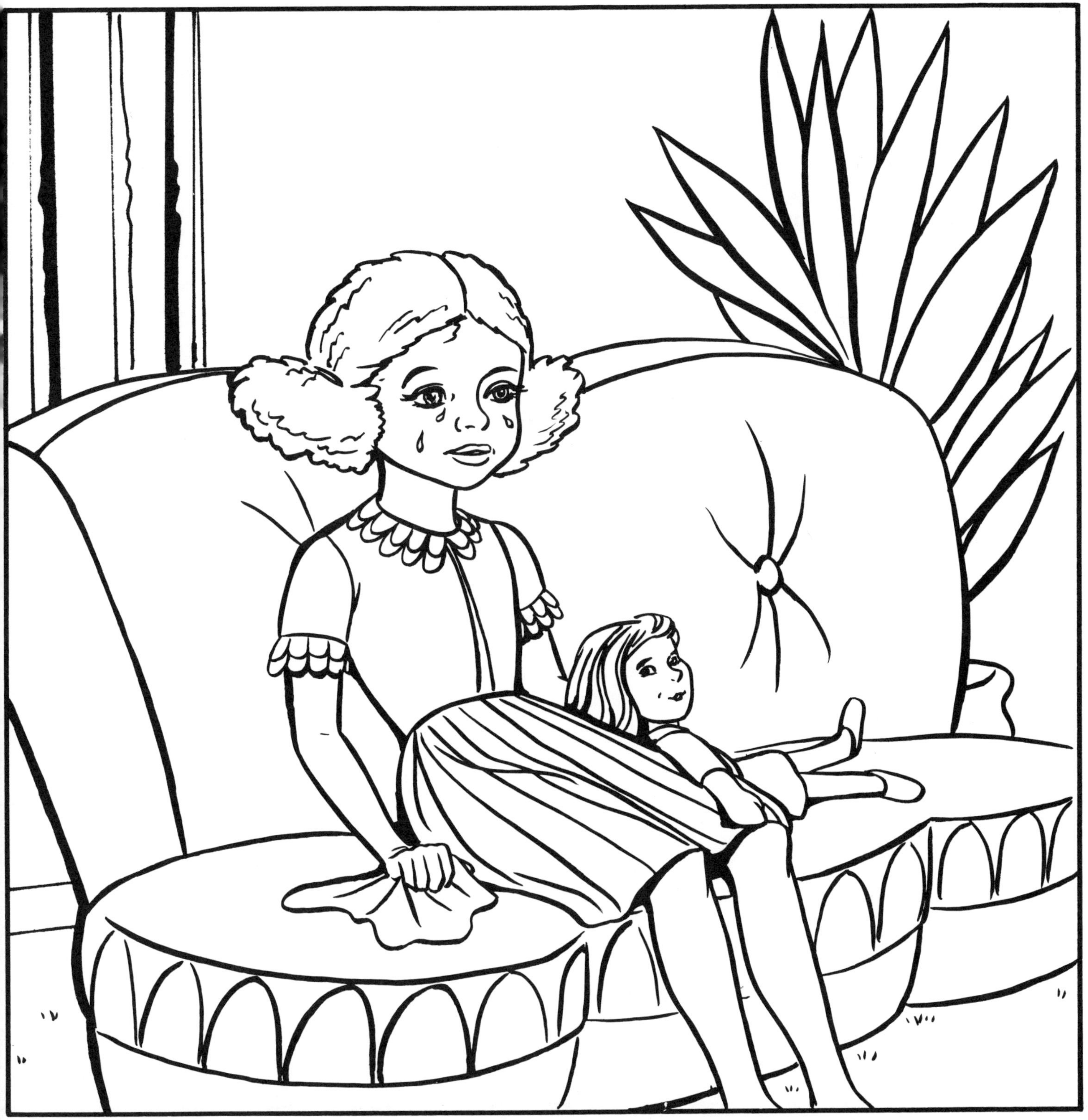

PARROT: (Squawk!) What's the trouble? You look rather down, rather down.

★★ **Who said that?**

PARROT: I did. (Squawk!)

★★ **Where are you?**

PARROT: Over here in the cage, in the cage.

★★ **The parrot?**

PARROT: In the feathers. (Squawk!)

★★ **I thought you could only say "Polly" things.**

PARROT: Poor Mark, poor Mark!

★★ **It doesn't matter, anyway.**

PARROT: Mark's sad, Mark's sad.

★★ **Why shouldn't I be? I don't have any friends.**

PARROT: You have one friend, a special friend.

★★ **Who?**

PARROT: I can't tell (Squawk!), but he's as big as you, and he's somebody your age.

★★ **I don't have a friend like that.**

PARROT: Oh (Squawk!), distressing, distressing! I know you have a friend like that someplace. (Squawk!) Let's go find him. Come into my cage and take my wing, take my wing.

★★ **But I can't get in. Well, maybe if I squeeze.**

PARROT: You can make it, (Squawk! Squawk!)

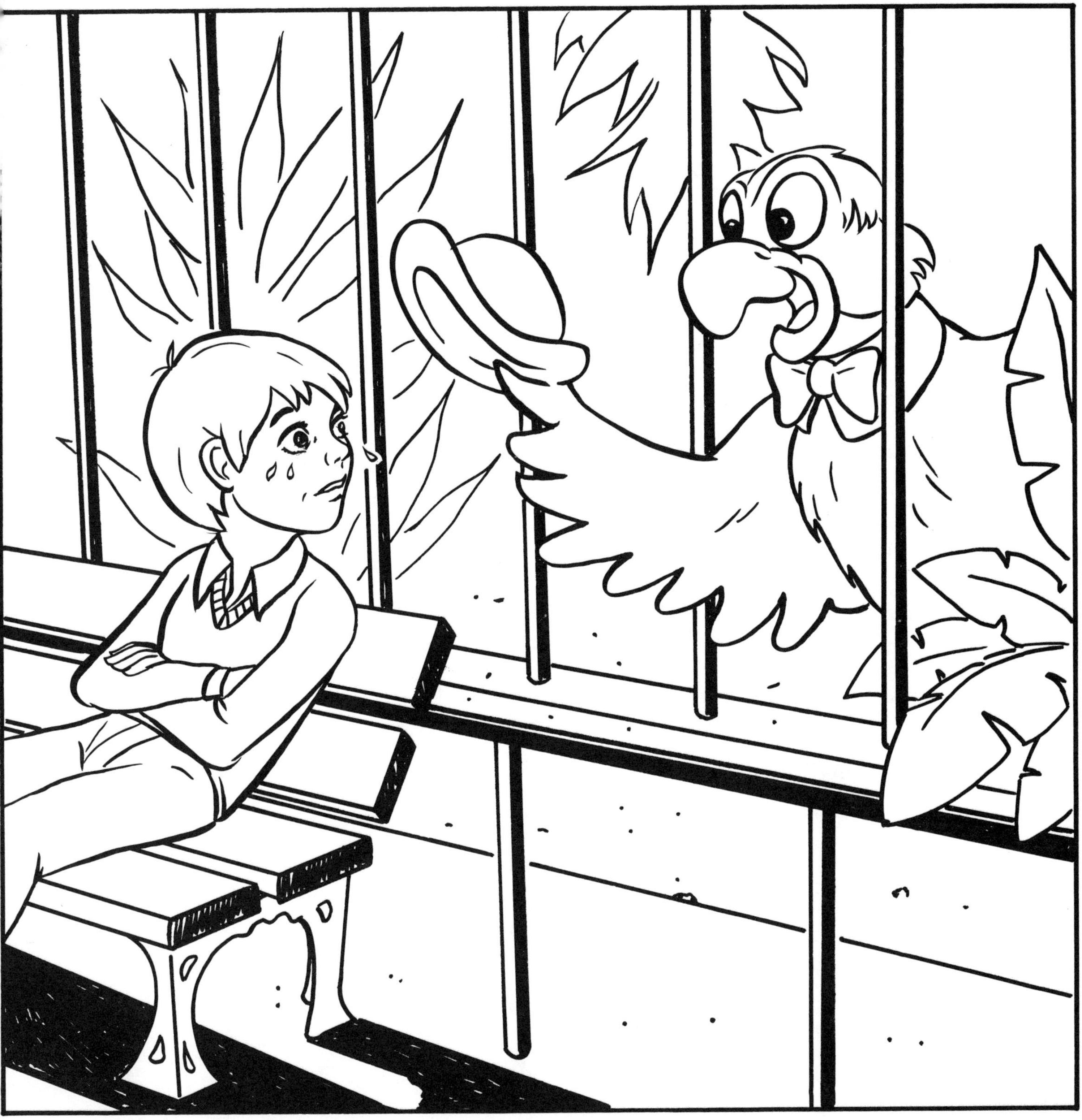

★★**This looks like the jungle.**

    PARROT: But, of course! I live in the jungle.

★★**Let's ask around and see if anyone has seen my special friend.**

    PARROT: (Squawk!) Great idea, great idea.

★★**What's that?**

    PARROT: It's a hippopotamus.

> Give a hip, hip hooray for the hippo, lazyin' in the sun.
> Give a hip, hip hooray for the hippo, seldom has any fun.
> Have a heart, have a heart for the hippo; she's as sad as she can be.
> When you're built this wide, there's no place to hide.
> You're just out where the world can see.

    PARROT: Ask her, Mark. Don't be shy, don't be shy.

★★**But I can't speak Hippopotamus. Oh, well. Excuse me, Miss Hippopotamus, have you seen my special friend? I don't know what he looks like, but he's my friend, and I'd like to find him.**

    HIPPO: How am I supposed to see anyone else? I'm so fat all I can possibly do is worry about myself. And even if I did lose all this weight, I'm not exactly what you'd call a beauty.

    PARROT: Tell her, Mark, you don't have to be skinny (Squawk!) or have a pretty face to feel good about yourself, about yourself.

★★**That's right! And what about all the nice things you do for others?**

    HIPPO: Nice things? What nice things?

★★**Well, like you let all those little birds ride on your back. They get a soft, warm place to rest even when there aren't any trees.**

    HIPPO: Oh, that is nice, isn't it!

★★**I bet they think you're a great hippopotamus.**

    HIPPO: Do you think so?

★★**I'm sure of it.**

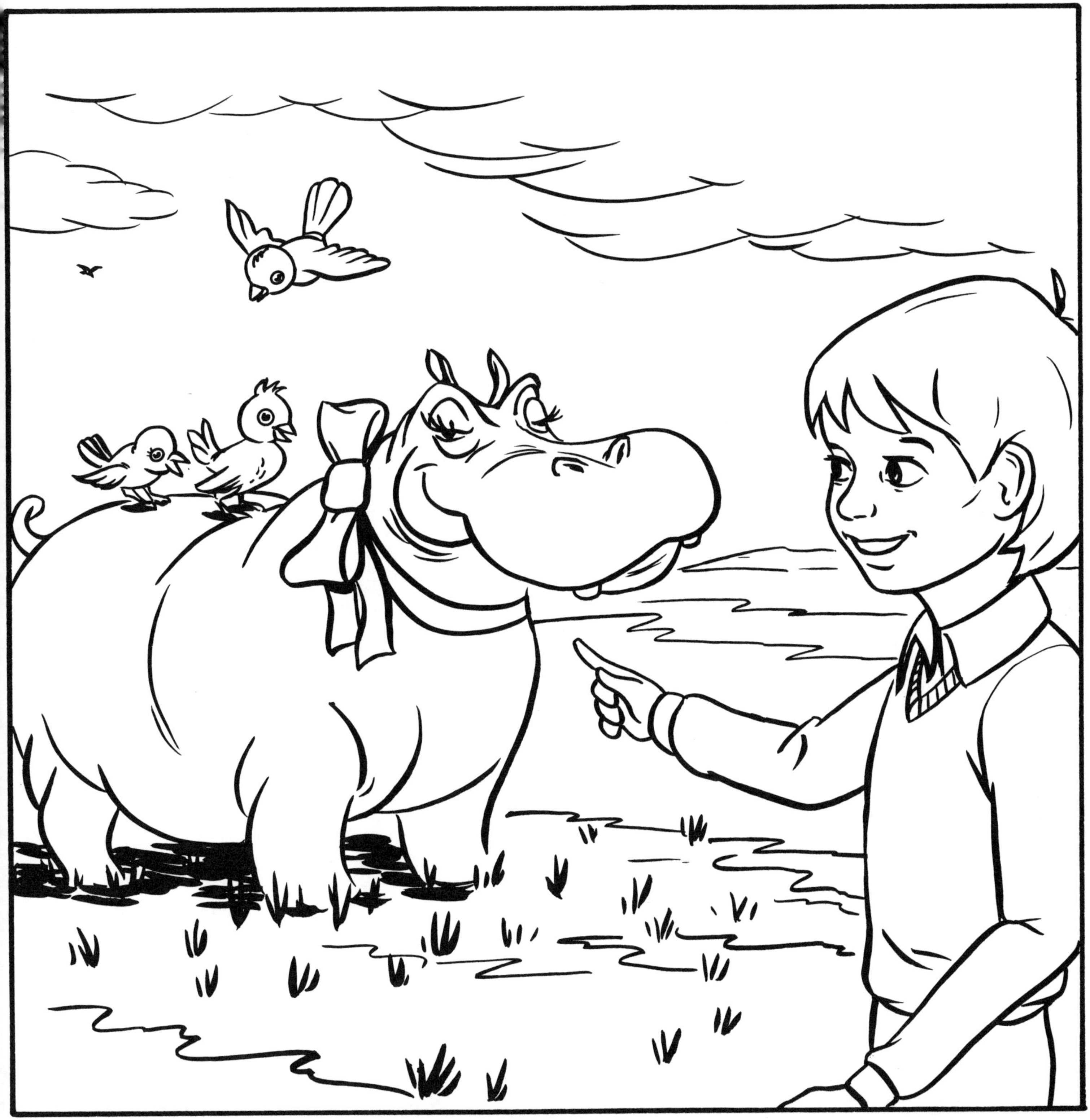

HIPPO: Oh, my goodness, I never imagined! Oh, I'm so happy you came by, Mark. I really had no idea that anyone liked me at all. My goodness. Oh, my goodness, I just can't wait to tell the girls!

♪♪ Have a heart, have a heart for me, the hippo; I won't ever be sad again.
When you're built this wide, there's a place to ride
For each little feathered friend. Girls, girls....

★ **Is it true you don't have to be pretty to have people like you?**

What do you think?

★ **Well, one of my friends is pretty, and everyone likes her a lot. But one of my other friends isn't really pretty, and everyone likes her, too.**

Why do people like her?

★ **She's fun and she's nice. She makes other people feel good. But tell me the rest of the story. Then what happened to Mark?**

Mark was afraid he'd never find his special friend; the jungle was very big. But the parrot had an idea.

PARROT: Hop on my back, Mark, on my back. Let's fly.

★★ **Where are we going?**

PARROT: You'll see, you'll see. I know exactly where we're going. (Squawk!) We're coming to a lake any minute, now. In fact—

★★ **Oh, do be careful!**

PARROT: (Squawk!) Big lake, big lake. Oh, dear!

★★ **We're falling. H-e-e-e-l-p!**

PARROT: Are you all right, all right?

★★ **I'm rather wet. Well, soaked, actually.**

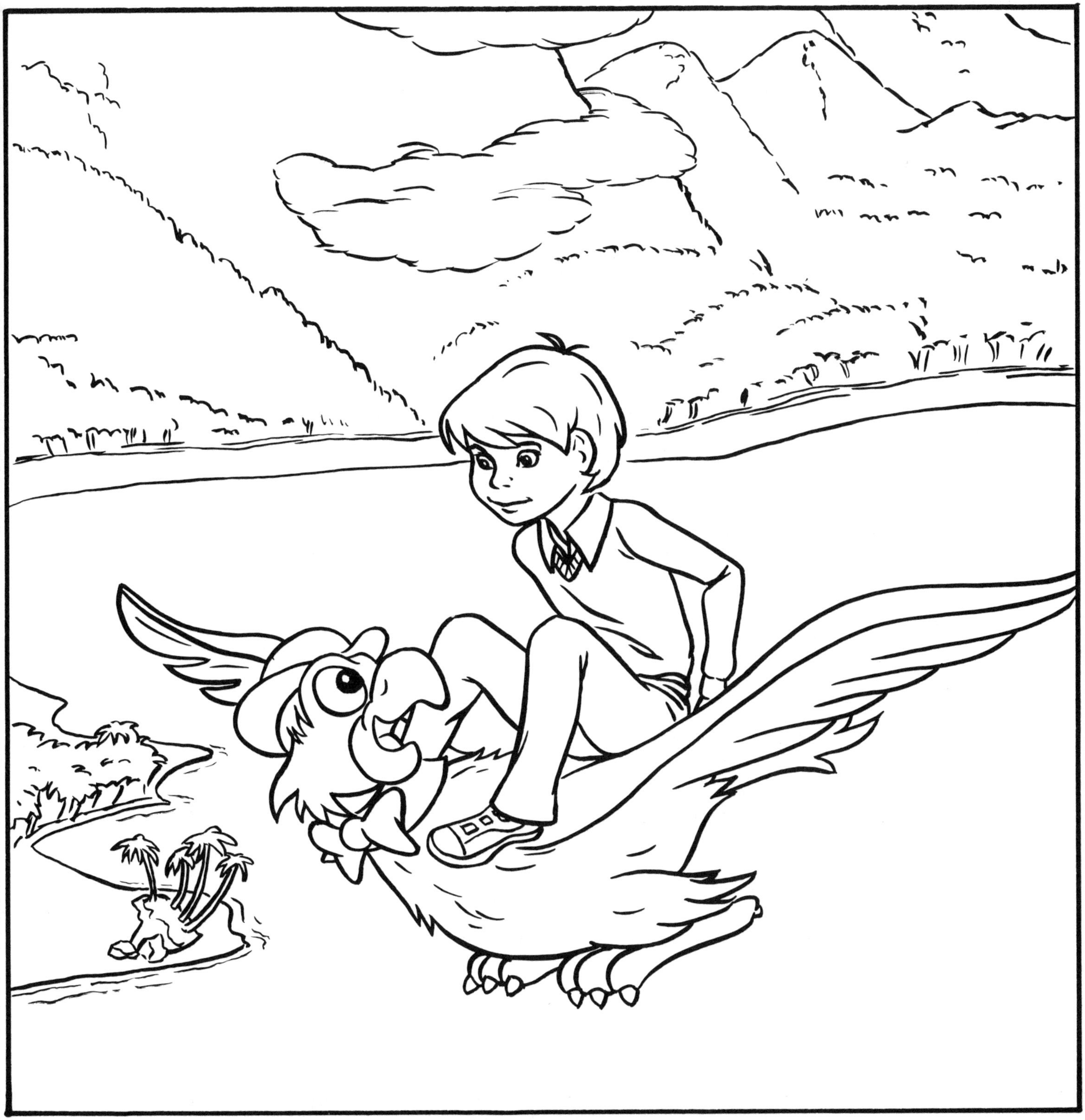

PARROT: As long as we're here, we might as well make the best of it. Maybe your friend is here.

★★ **Underwater?**

PARROT: Why not, why not?

★★ **I just never thought—look, a school of fish. They're beautiful! So many of them! That's strange, they all move at the same time.**

FISH: What funny creatures! Not a scale.
    Are they fish? I can't tell.

PARROT: (Squawk!) I am a parrot, and this is Mark. He is a boy. (Squawk!)

FISH: Ah, visitors! Just dropped in.
    How nice! Can you swim?

★★ **I'm looking for my special friend. He's a lot of fun. I'm sure you'd like him. Has he been here?**

FISH: We couldn't tell. We're all the same.
    We look alike, it's very plain.

★★ **You mean you all do exactly the same thing all the time?**

FISH: That's right, how true!
    We act alike, yes, we do.

★★ **But nothing can be exactly like anything else. Each of you has to be different.**

FISH: Not us. No, sir-ee.
    In what way? Couldn't be.

★★ **Well, your voices. Some are high and some are low.**

FISH: Impossible! Oh, no!
    Preposterous! Isn't so.

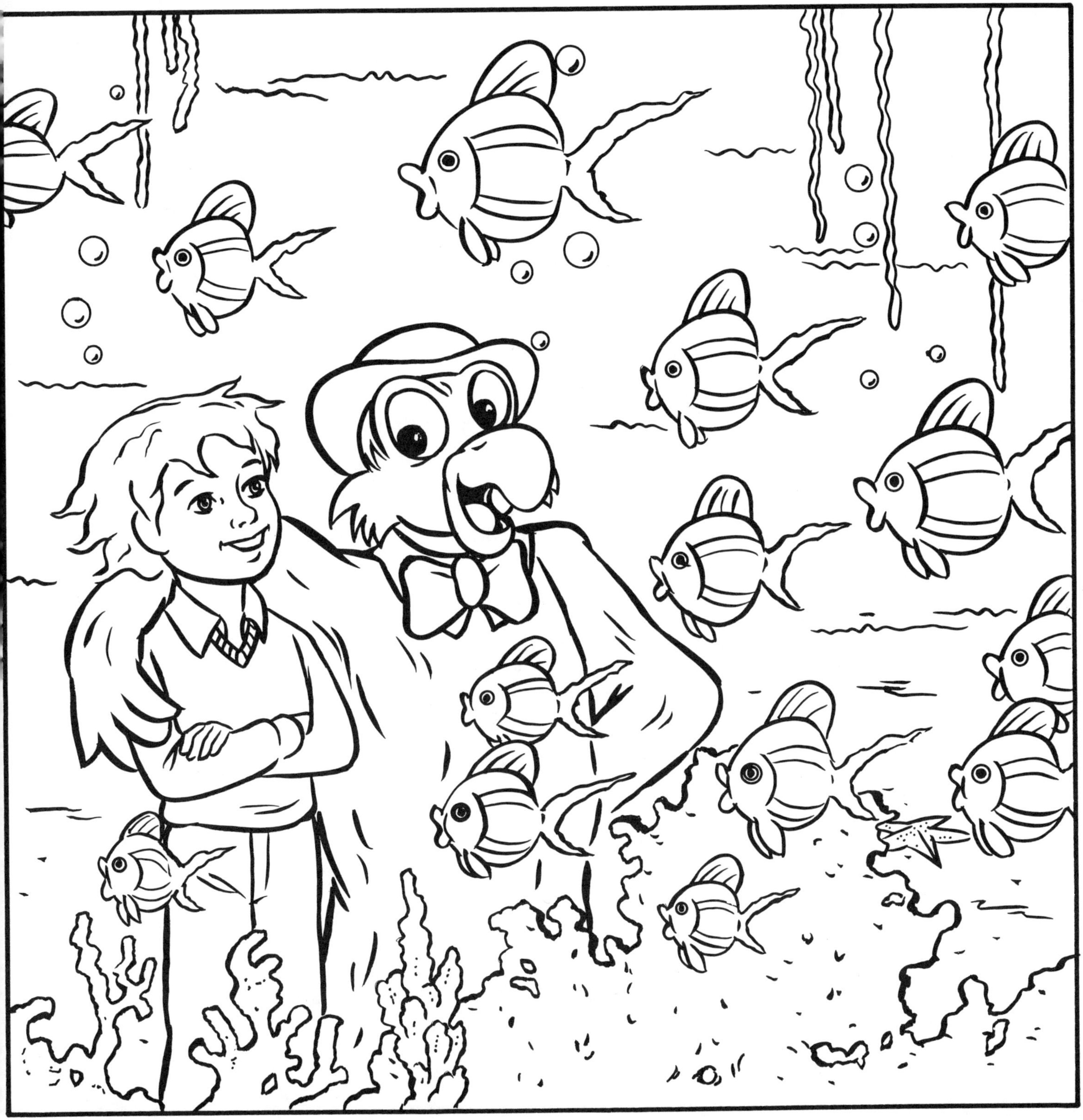

★★**But it's true. Say "fish" one at a time.**

FISH: Fish, fish, fish, fish, tuna.
We're different, we're different!
How exciting!
How wonderful!
Stupendous!

Thought that we were all the same, but we're not, but we're not.
We're different, we're different.
Thought that it would be a shame, but it's not, but it's not,
To be different, to be different.

We all swim left, then we all swim right.
Keeping in the swim was keeping me uptight.
We all conform to the fishy school.
Now there's a brand new fishy in the fishy pool.

Thought I had to be like you, but I don't, but I don't—
I'm different, I'm different—
Doing everything you do. Now I won't, now I won't,
Because I'm different, because I'm different.

And on one thing we agree:
What's happy for you's not always happy for me.
There's a billion fishies in the sea,
But there's not another fish like me.
Different, different, everybody's different.
Different, different, everybody's different.
Different, different, everybody's different.

★**I try so hard to be like my friends, to look like them and do everything they do, but I just can't do it.**

Of course you can't! And they can't be like you.

★**And is it all right to be different?**

Yes, it's all right, Emily.

★**Next time Camille says, "Let's ride bikes," and I want to read, would it be okay to read?**

I think it would be just fine.

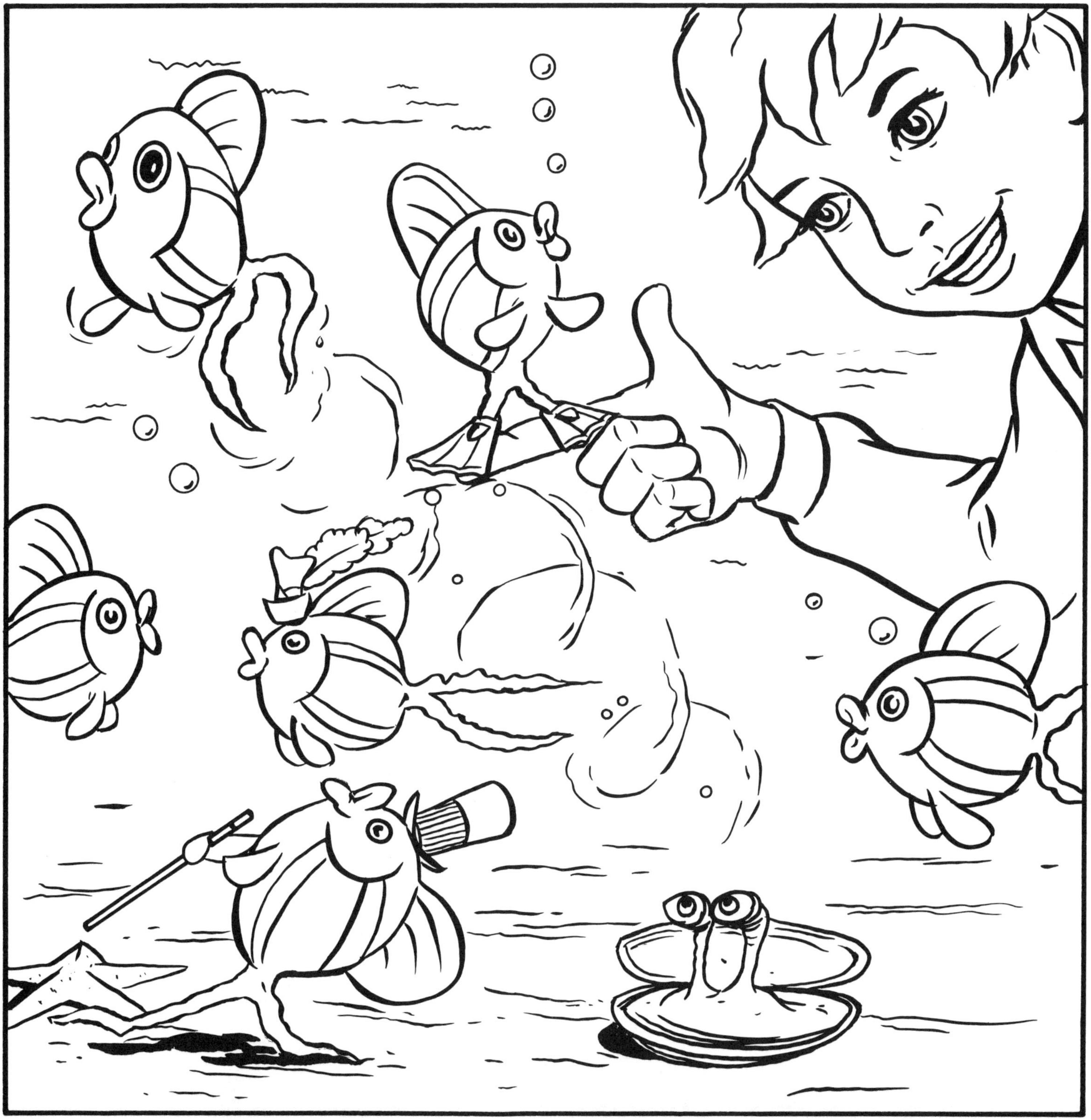

★I don't have to be like other people to make them like me. That's nice to know. I can just be me.

 There's just one little nose like mine.
It belongs to me.
And these two little eyes that shine,
They're my specialty.

One little mouth distinctly mine upon my face.
One little chin—no other like it anyplace.

There's just one little voice like mine
Anywhere you go—
One little voice, and when it talks,
It is me, you know.

I'm a singular person, one of a kind.
There's not another like me
You could ever, ever find.

★★My friend is close, I can feel it.

PARROT: I think you're right, Mark, right, Mark.

★★What's all that noise up there in the trees? Do you hear it?

PARROT: Oh, dear (Squawk!), I think we're surrounded, surrounded.

★★It's monkeys! They're as big as I am.

BONO: Hey, kid, wanna play? Take off your shoes and join us for an afternoon swing through the trees.

GORF: Bono, he's got funny looking toes, and he doesn't have a tail. How can he swing?

BONO: Oh, pardon me. I'm so embarrassed!

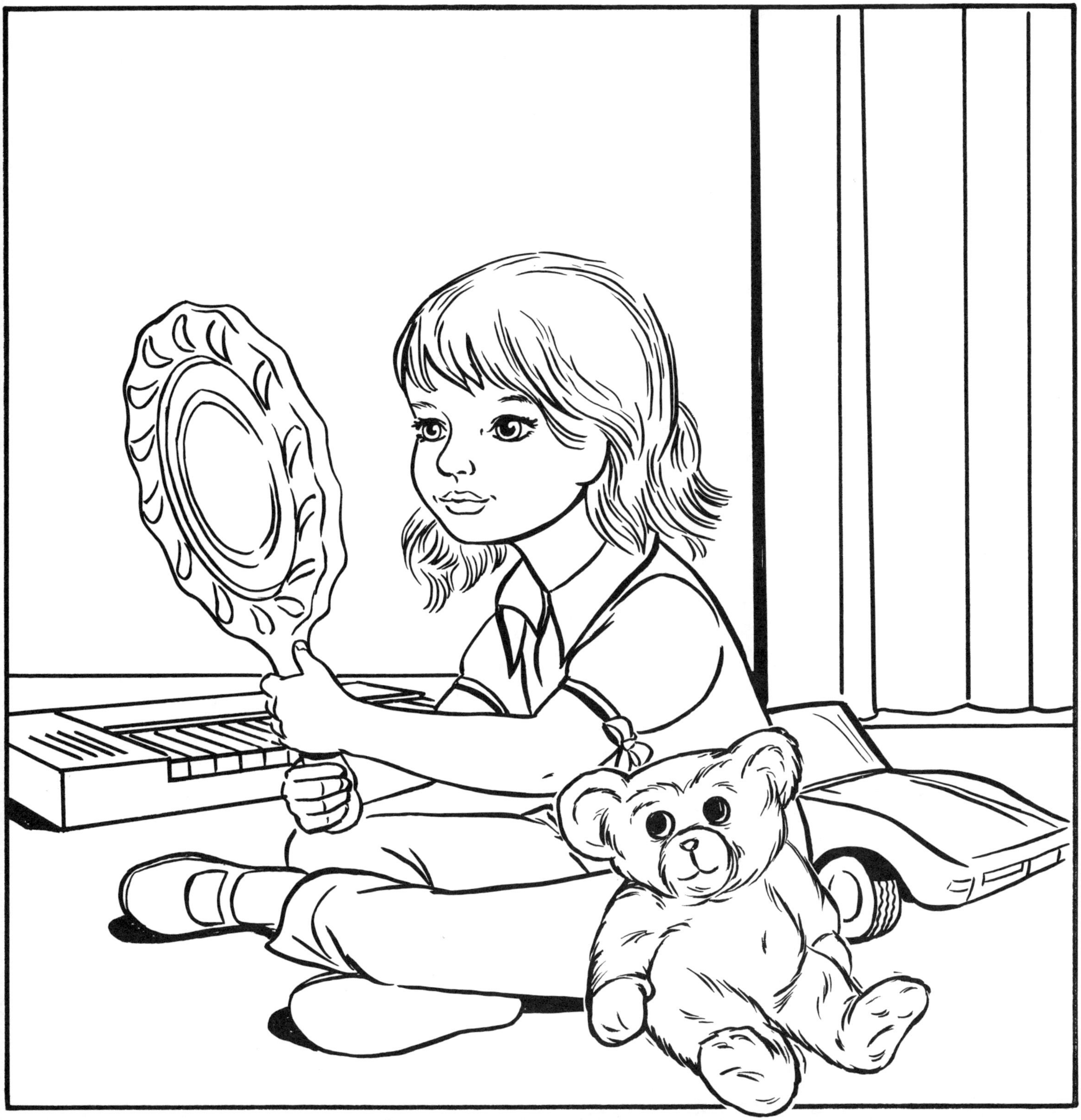

★★I wish I could swing, but I'm looking for my special friend. Have any of you seen him? He's my size and he looks a lot like me.

BONO: Doesn't he have a tail either?

GORF: That's not a nice thing to say.

BONO: Oh, you're right. I'm so embarrassed!

GORF: We monkeys don't notice much. We spend most of our time hiding our faces. We're always doing dumb things.

BONO: You don't need to tell him all our troubles.

GORF: You're right. Oh, I'm so embarrassed!

♪ Oh, I'm so embarrassed, oh, I'm so embarrassed!
How could I ever do such a clumsy thing?
They'll never for— never for— never for— never forgive you.
(That was a clumsy thing to do !)
I've made a mi— made a mi— made a mistake again.
(Aren't you embarrassed?)

Oh, I'm so embarrassed, oh, I'm so embarrassed!
How could I ever act such a stupid way?
I hope they don't, hope they don't, hope they don't ever remember.
(That was a stupid way to act.)
I'll never dare, never dare, never dare face them again.

I do the wrong thing. I go the wrong way.
Can't think of a name. I forget what to say.
I made another boo-boo today.
I trip on my foot. I drop what I hold.
I stop and I stare. I forget what I'm told.
I made another boo-boo today.
It's so exasperating, awfully devastating,
Quite intimidating, very complicating.

Oh, I'm so embarrassed, oh, I'm so embarrassed!
How could I ever say such a silly thing?
I wonder if, wonder if, wonder if they will still like you.
(That was a silly thing to say.)
I goofed it up, goofed it up, goofed it up badly again.
It's too humiliating, so incriminating,
Madly aggravating, socially degrading.
Oh, I'm so embarrassed!

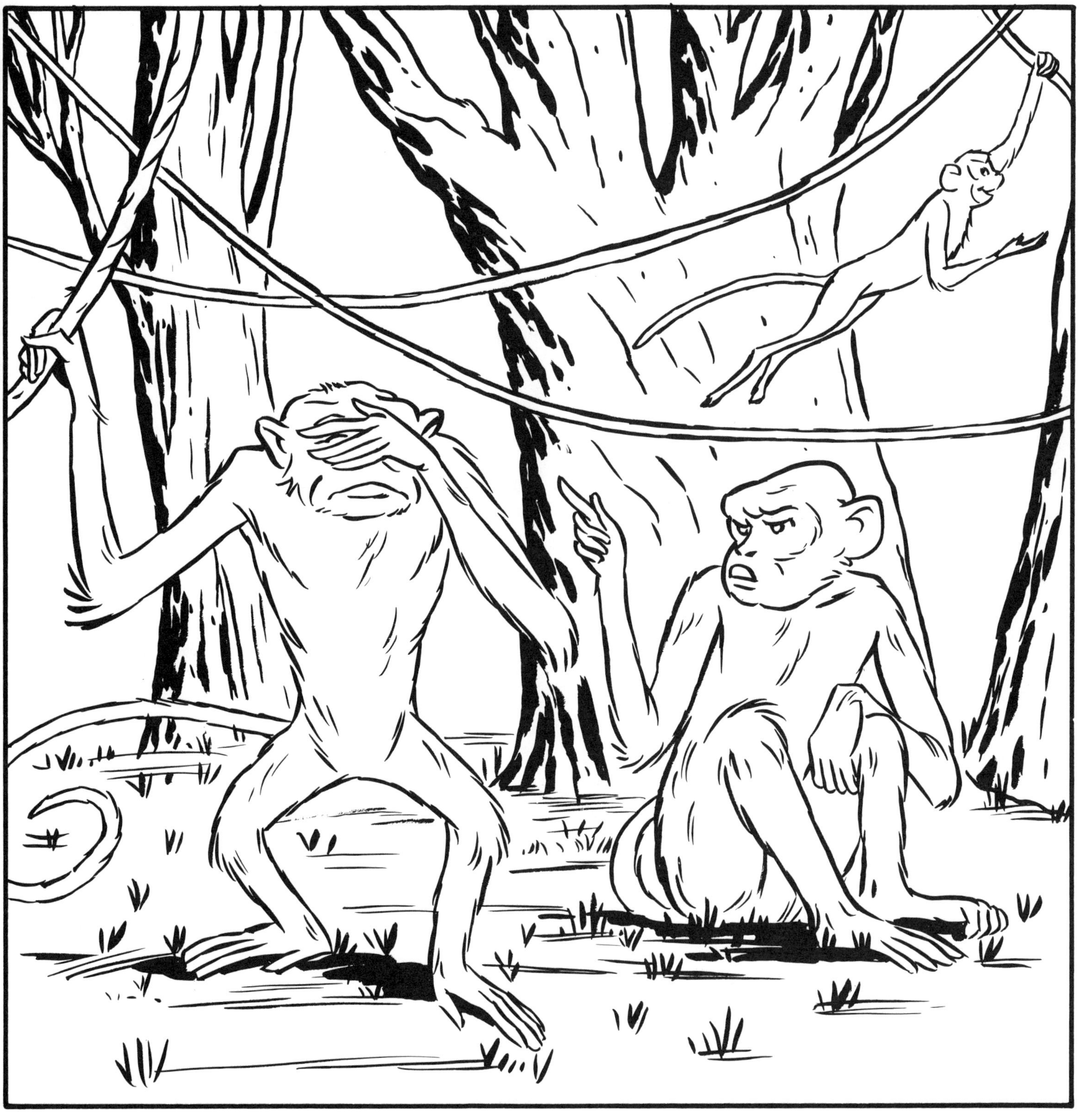

★★Hey, you guys, everyone does things that are silly sometimes. We all make mistakes.

GORF: Really?

BONO: No kidding?

★★But you have to forget about the silly things you do and remember the things you do right. You don't need to be embarrassed all the time.

BONO: But what will everybody think?

★★They'll forget, too, if you let them.

★That's the whole problem. Today at school I had to read in front of the class. I got all mixed up and everybody laughed, and now I'm afraid they don't like me.

I'm sure that's upsetting to you. But you know how well you read, and your teacher knows. Let's think about the things you did right today.

★Well—I turned in my assignment on time, and I shared a swing at recess.

And all you've been remembering is the mistake you made.

★I think I'm beginning to understand. I shouldn't worry about what I do wrong as long as I'm trying to do right. I like the story about Mark and the funny parrot. Did he find his special friend?

He surely did. Those monkeys were having so much fun, Mark couldn't just stand around and watch.

★★Boy, that looks fun, swinging through those trees. Can I try it?

PARROT: Try it, try it (Squawk!), but be careful.

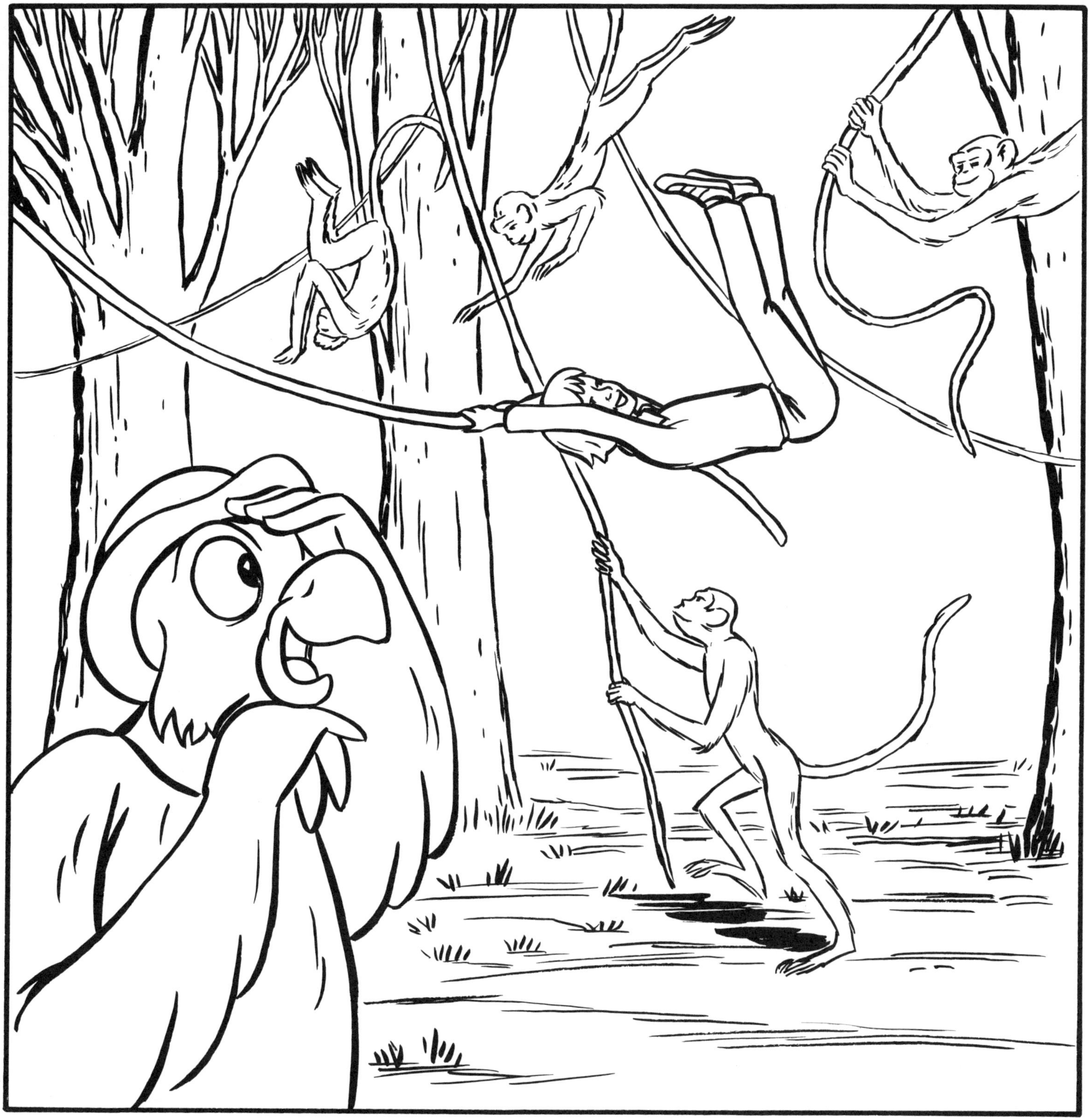

MONKEYS: Mark's coming up. Great! Come on, give him a lift. Up you go!

GORF: Grab this vine and you're off.

★★**How's this for not having a tail? Whee!**

BONO: Oh, dear!

PARROT: (Squawk!) He's slipping, he's slipping! Catch that boy!

MONKEYS: I'll get him, I'll get him, he's mine, I got him, I got him. Oops!

★★**I'm okay. I landed on the moss by the pond. I can see my reflection. It's him! I found him, my friend! It's me. I'm my friend!**

PARROT: Smart boy (Squawk!), smart boy.

I'm my friend, my very special friend.
And I'll always try and be
The kind of person who can like myself, see myself
Honestly, honestly.

I'm my friend, my very special friend.
And, no matter where I go,
I'll always look to see
The fine and good in me, for then
I'll be happy with my special friend.

★**Can I be my friend, too?**

I hope so. You must like yourself first, and then other people will like you.

★**And it doesn't matter if I'm not really beautiful or if I'm different, or even if I make mistakes. I can still do good things and make other people happy. I can still feel good about me.**

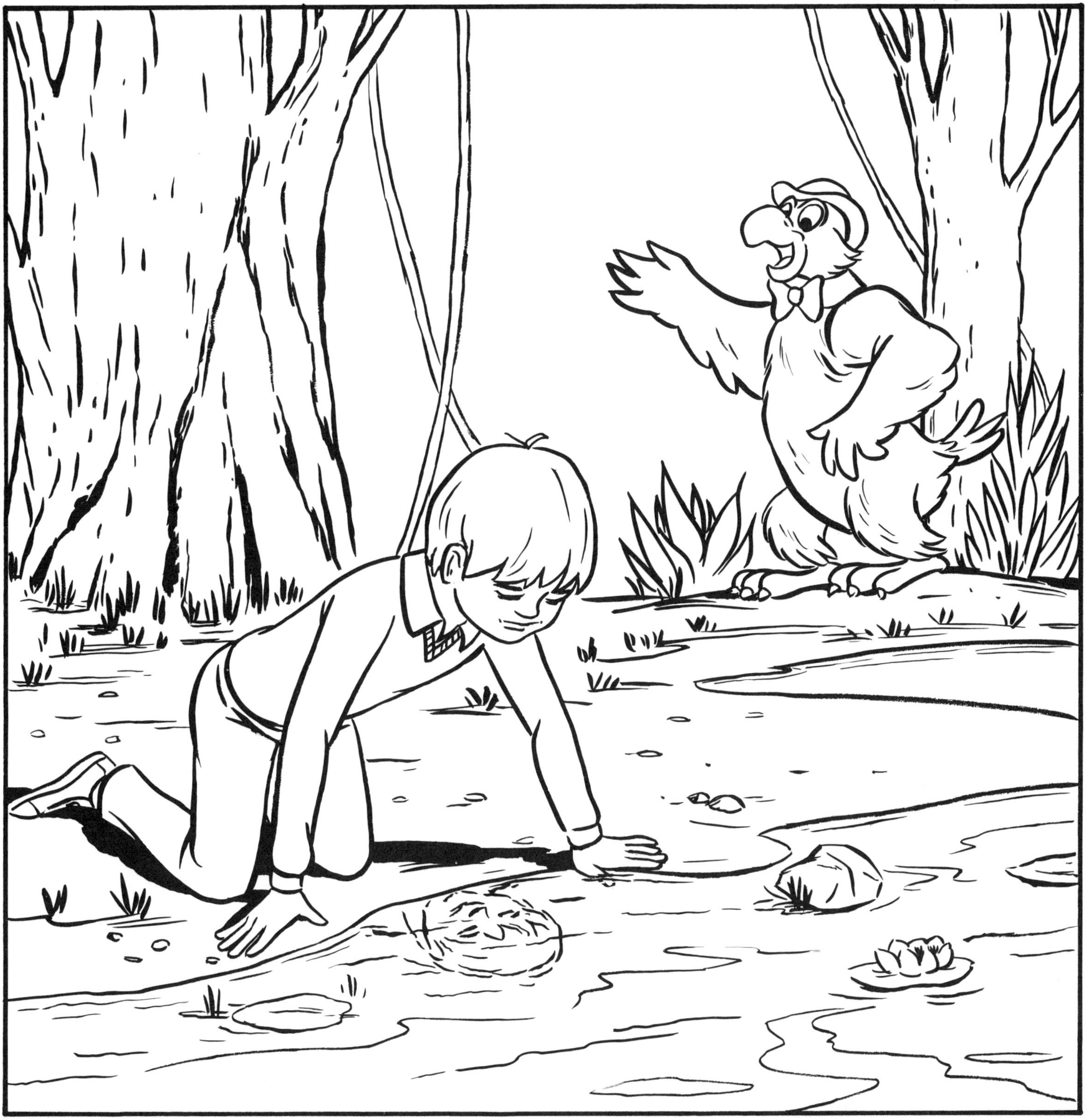

I've a friend, very close to me,
Someone who likes me.
When I think no one cares for me,
My friend is helping me to see

I'm worthwhile, I am very rare,
There's no one like me.
And it's nice knowing that you care,
My special friend.

Now may I ask you a question?

★ **If you want to.**

Pretend there was a new child at school you had never met. What would they like about you when they got to know you?

★ **Would it be bragging if I told?**

Not at all. Now, think. What's special about you?

★ **Well, I do smile a lot.**

Yes, you do. Would you make a list of the things that make you feel good about yourself? I'd really like that.

★ **Okay, that sounds fun.**

I've a friend, very close to me,
Someone who likes me.
When I think no one cares for me,
My friend is helping me to see

I'm worthwhile, I am very rare,
There's no one like me.
And it's nice knowing that you care,
My special friend.

I'm my friend, my very special friend.
And I'll always try and be
The kind of person who can like myself, see myself
Honestly, honestly.

I'm my friend, my very special friend.
And, no matter where I go,
I'll always look to see
The fine and good in me, for then
I'll be happy with my special friend.

★ **Now I'm going to make my list of all the good things about me. And do you know what would be nice—if all children would make their own lists! Then they will all know how special they are.**

That would be wonderful!

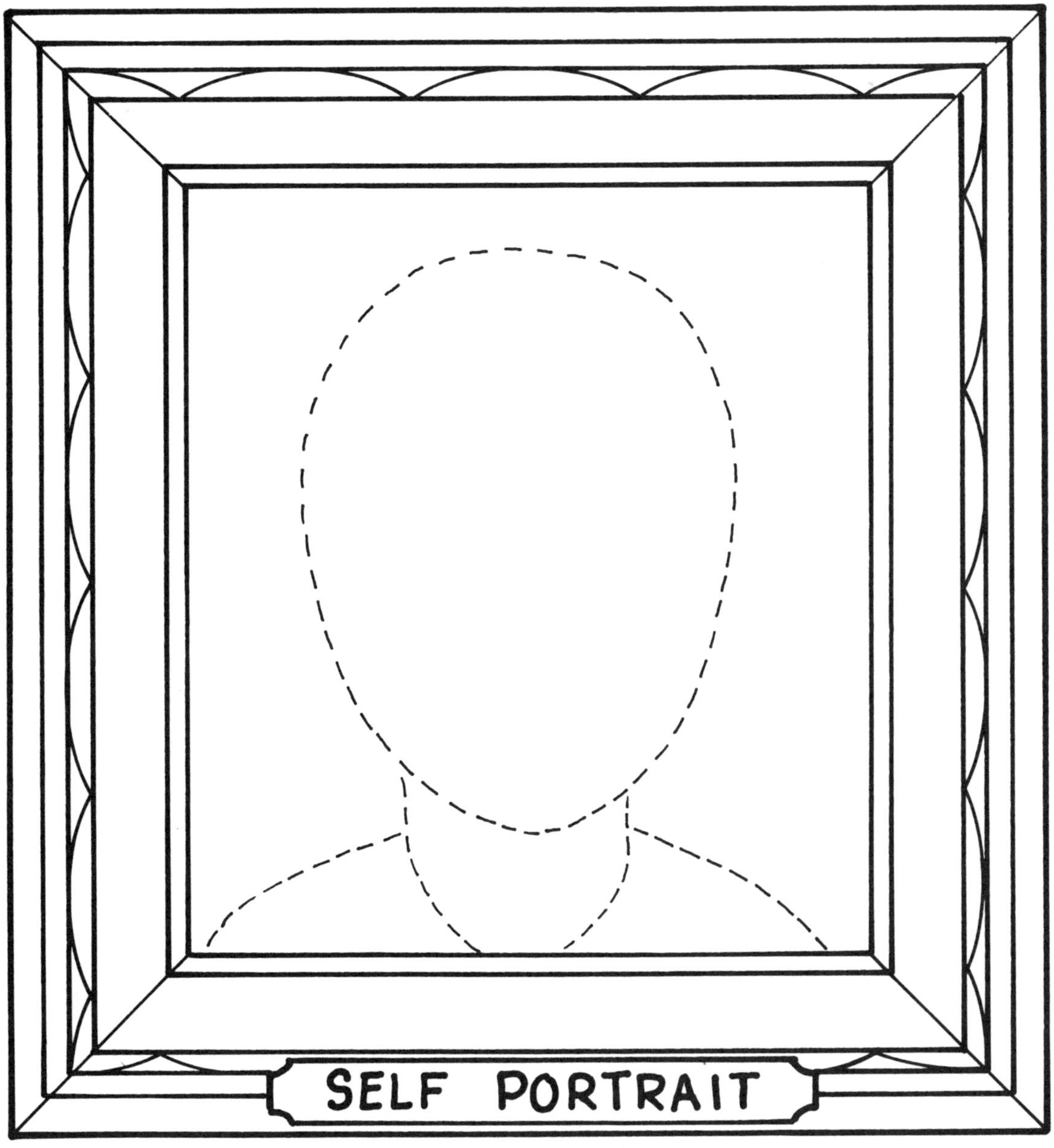
SELF PORTRAIT

I Am A Special Person

Side A of each cassette contains the complete program. **Side B** repeats the same program but leaves out the lines of the main child in the story, giving the listener the chance to read along, saying aloud the missing lines and actually becoming a member of the cast. This fascinating activity helps older children with their reading and provides an excellent opportunity for development in dramatics.

Children can sing along with the songs, color the pictures and participate in still other activities as the story progresses.

A Product of BRITE MUSIC ENTERPRISES, INC.

Music and Dramatics recorded, engineered and mixed at Bonneville Media Communications.
Illustrations by Grant Wilson / Graphic production by Whipple & Associates.
Music arranged and conducted by Merrill Jenson.